The Mantra of Adoga

Profound Practices for Personal Growth

Ryan C. Taylor

© 2023 Ryan Taylor

All Rights Reserved.

ISBN: 978-1-7324819-6-1

Check out Ryan's other books and projects at:

projectado.com

Contents

Introduction

The Path of the Profound Mantra • 7

The Intentions of this Book • 10

Incorporating Many Perspectives • 12

Fundamental Practices

Relax and Create • 14

Listen to Your Gut, Heart, and Head • 17

Relax, Receive, Create • 20

Observational Practices

Observe Your Breathing • 22

Observe Your Thinking • 22

Witness in Freedom • 23

Find Stillness • 23

A Sequence in Four Steps

Relax, Feel, Observe, Create • 25

Release and Expression • 27

Imaginative Practices

Simple Imagination • 29

Positive and Negative Imagination • 30

Imagine Something Unexpected • 31

Intention-Based Practices

An Emotion, Mindset, and Goal • 32

Overcome a Psychological Block • 34

Bring Your Intention into Your Day-to-Day Life • 36

The Full Spectrum

Relax, Feel, Observe, Imagine, Intend • 37

Simple Alignment Method • 40

Meditate on the Four Elements

Earth • 42

Water • 43

Fire • 43

Air • 44

Earth Transformed • 44

Visioning Your Future – Part I • 45

Discovering Shadows

The Integral Developmental Spectrum • 46

The Enneagram of Personality • 50

Shadows in the Adoga Spectrum • 59

Visioning Your Future – Part II • 64

The Emotions of the Adoga Spectrum

Alignment Method Based on Emotions • 65

Relax – Tiredness and Readiness • 66

Feel – Hurt and Love • 66

Observe – Depression and Peace • 68

Imagine – Fear and Inspiration • 69

Intend – Anger and Power • 70

Directions for Alignment Method • 72

Relax, Feel, & Release More • 75

The Psychology of the Adoga Spectrum

Alignment Method Based on Thoughts • 78

Using Relaxation as a Fun Foundation • 78

Feel Your Way to Forgiveness • 81

Five Step Forgiveness • 82

Observe Your Way to Hope and Vast Possibility • 86

Imagine and Intend Your Way to the Future • 88

A Summary for Alignment Method • 90

Intellectual Practices and Techniques

Chunking Big and Small • 91

Probability and Logical Fallacies • 95

Don't Throw the Baby Out with the Bathwater • 98

Thinking for Yourself • 100

Search for the Opposite • 101

Discovery Journaling • 102

Integration

Formulating Your Constitution • 105

Relax and Create • 106

Making It Physical • 107

Visioning Your Future – Part III • 109

Conclusion

The Resilient Mantra • 110

The Inspirations of Adoga • 112

Acknowledgements, Sources, and Gratitude • 114

Introduction

The Path of the Profound Mantra

One who fears the future, who fears failure, limits his activities. Failure is only the opportunity more intelligently to begin again. There is no disgrace in honest failure; there is disgrace in fearing to fail. What is past is useful only as it suggests ways and means for progress.

– Henry Ford, *My Life and Work*

This book offers a series of personal growth practices based on different forms of meditation, psychological techniques, and philosophical perspectives. Each practice contains a powerful potential to enhance and transform your emotional wellbeing, intellectual capacity, and connection to the wonderous meaning of life. Furthermore, when we are able to improve our inner world, we are more able to create the outer world that we desire. In this sense, these practices are about more than *feeling* good. They are about creating the life you desire and sharing your gifts with the world.

From the practices, a philosophy of life emerges. To begin with, this philosophy is the path of the profound mantra. A mantra is something that one repeats and focuses on during meditation. However, if the mantra were only repetition, it would not produce growth. Therefore, the more profound kind of mantra is one where something stays the same and something else changes. We could think of the part that stays the same as order and the part that changes as chaos. It is the skillful combination of order and chaos which produces creative and novel advancements into a brighter future.

The mantra points to the anchoring and stabilizing virtues of repetition. To learn, we must repeat. We must try again and again. We must persist. The effort of repetition is sometimes difficult. Inevitably, it involves the pain of failure. And yet, without repeated, sustained effort toward a goal, we are lost and depressed. The hope of a better future ignites our sense of purpose and meaning.

Eastern philosophy often points to the peace and mysterious beauty that emerges from letting go of goals, thinking, distinctions, and all manner of structures that we generally rely on in our day-to-day lives. While this insight can be deeply important, it is incomplete on its own. Letting go provides rest and, at times, offers unique insights. However, we must return to our goals again and again, for this gives life greater purpose. In our practices, we will use both deconstructive techniques which involve letting go of old emotions, beliefs, and goals as well as reconstructive techniques which involve the creation of new emotions, beliefs, and goals.

The philosophy of the mantra brings with it many virtues: hope, courage, persistence, patience, and faith. Faith, as I use the term here, does not refer to the blind faith that entails believing without cause. Rather, the more sophisticated conception of faith that I refer to here is the commitment to act in alignment with what you know to be right. Faith is our guide when the most moral decision causes us to waver, when the right thing to do causes us to doubt or dwell upon the sacrifices required of us. Faith is the inexhaustible resource that says:

Yes, I will try yet again regardless – regardless of the past, the failures, the betrayals, the sense of inadequacy, the fear of destruction, regardless of all the reasons not to try again.

Faith is depression inverted.

If we can anchor ourselves in the hopeful stability of the mantra, a world of exploration will open up to us. With order as an ally, chaos transforms from the unbearable turmoil of the sea into the joyful surfing of the ever-evolving and ever-fascinating waves.

The Intentions of this Book

This book centers on personal growth practices. I will share activities that you can incorporate into your inwardly focused time, whether you think of that time as meditation, prayer, contemplation, self-development, or some other similar concept. You can also treat these practices as a step-by-step course or progression into your own psyche. Taken together, these practices create a natural growth arc and can help you to create an inspiring new phase in your life, guided by meaningful goals, empowering emotions, and useful insights.

Although we will explore deep ideas, this book starts at the very beginning and does not require any prior knowledge of meditation, psychology, or any related subject. All you need is a desire to grow and a willingness to try the practices.

Occasionally, I will include brief adventures into philosophical or intellectual content related to the practices. Though, these departures will be kept to a minimum to emphasize the focus on practices.

I encourage you to use a journal to describe important experiences you encounter while going through this book. Some of the practices involve writing exercises. Your journal can become a valuable tool for capturing and organizing your light bulb moments and psychological journey throughout this process.

I will often guide you through practices in a somewhat poetic tone. In these sections, you may want to periodically stop reading and dedicate your attention to meditating upon or executing the practice that I am describing. You can even stop after each sentence and spend a minute exploring that specific intention or idea.

I will sometimes repeat the practices in different variations or sequences. This is intended to help you master the relevant skills from many different angles. I encourage you to embrace each repetition and variation as a new opportunity to discover, learn, and grow.

Please, consider making a commitment to practice the techniques in this book for a given duration (perhaps 15 minutes to start) at a consistent time (perhaps in the morning before you start your day). Commitments of this nature can be helpful for forming good habits and solidifying your progress.

Incorporating Many Perspectives

It is important to draw wisdom from many different places. If you take it from only one place, it becomes rigid and stale. Understanding others, the other elements, and the other nations, will help you become whole.

-Uncle Iroh in Avatar: The Last Airbender

Book 2, Episode 9: "Bitter Work"

Adoga is a method of personal growth that seeks to include the broadest, most diverse, most encompassing, and most foundational patterns of the human spirit. If we can cover the most ground possible, we will eliminate as many blind spots as possible. Therefore, we will explore different levels of the psyche, personality types, and other patterns that help us to become more and more aware. By investigating all these possibilities, we will progress toward ever-increasing levels of completeness, understanding, and empowerment.

In essence, Adoga is a collection of personal growth practices based on the biggest-picture patterns we can conceptualize and work with. (See the section entitled "The Inspirations of Adoga" on page 112 for more information about the Adoga framework.)

We will begin with just two, very foundational, practices: relaxation and creation.

Fundamental Practices

Relax and Create

We begin with relaxation, and there is something very important about that. We start by letting go of our intentions to see if any of them were unnecessary or harmful.

Try it now. Take a deep breath and relax yourself. Relax your muscles, your thoughts, your feelings. Relax it all. Let go of any effort you feel comfortable letting go of.

Imagine water washing you clean. Relaxation cleans your heart and mind. Cleaning means to wash away the dirt. Let the dirt represent all the intentions and emotions that do not serve you. Perhaps your dirt is stress. Perhaps it is anger. Or perhaps it is sadness and tiredness.

You can imagine these old, unnecessary emotions flowing out of you into the ground. Imagine a connection with the Earth that grounds you and metabolizes all that you no longer need.

Relax. Relax deeper each time you repeat this intention. Let yourself drift and see what that's like.

What is here when you stop exerting effort? Maybe, what's here is simple, restorative spaciousness. Or maybe what's here is everything you usually run away from, and maybe this is an opportunity to face those things.

Relaxation pulls away the dirt like a vacuum cleaner being pushed across a carpet. Direct your relaxation across each muscle, each sensation, each emotion, each intention.

Exhale and relax. Inhale and feel your body. Exhale and relax. Relax deeper each time.

Find space. Find stillness. Find the nothingness underneath every something.

Now, let's progress from relaxing to creating. Try moving your hand and notice what that feels like. You can move your hand in any direction you'd like. Continue moving your hand and notice yourself making choices in each movement. Notice the process of free will and its realization as real events in the physical world. Who is it that is directing your hand? Can you feel yourself? Can you feel your core self?

What else can you create with your beautiful intention? Can you imagine a circle or square?

Can you imagine a texture or sound? Can you imagine joy or love? Can you imagine giving love to others? Can you imagine giving love to yourself? Can you imagine a beautiful smile? Can you imagine yourself achieving an amazing goal?

How do such imaginations make you feel? When your mind creates, does your body respond? How do you feel right now?

Inhale and feel your body. Exhale and relax.

Each time we create, a little dirt is left behind and a little cleaning is called for. Let's relax again.

Let your imaginations go.

Let your intentions go.

Return to space. Return to the vacuum.

Vacuum turns into cleanliness. Cleanliness turns into organization. Organization turns into readiness.

Relax.

Now let's return to your physical world. How does your body feel? How does your environment look and sound?

Find completion and notice if you feel different now compared with your experience at the beginning of this practice.

The Pillars of Effort and Relaxation

Effort and relaxation are the two most basic pillars we can meditate upon. Action and the release of action. Intention and the release of intention. What we do and what we choose not to do. Creation and deconstruction. All choices and therefore all the significance of your life is tied to this duality. In the body, this truth can be felt symbolically as the effort it takes to expand the lungs and the relaxation which accompanies exhalation. Back and forth we must travel. In and out. Effort and relaxation.

Listen to Your Gut, Heart, and Head

Your gut, heart, and head all contain important nervous systems worth listening to. Each is continuously reporting important information.

Listening or receiving is the next practice that we will engage with. Listening – in its many forms – is incredibly important, because it is the only pathway through which new awareness can emerge.

Let's start by relaxing once again. I will almost always use relaxation as a way to establish foundations at the beginning of a practice and as a way to integrate novel insights and recover at the end of a practice.

When you are ready, turn your attention to your gut and the sensations around that area of your body. Listen to your body and notice if you feel any form of resistance. Resistances exist where information has been repressed. Repression takes effort and, thus, is exhausting. To un-repress, we must relax a specific effort which keeps information away from our awareness. Therefore, to listen more we must relax more while remaining attentive to the new information that emerges.

Again, let's relax and listen to the gut. What is there in this present moment? Can you relax any resistances that you might feel?

Let's relax and listen to the heart – the seat of so much emotion. Listen to the lungs as they breathe. Again, relax resistances and stay attentive to whatever you feel. Spend an extra moment carefully and curiously listening to the heart. Like a good friend, invite your heart to reveal its vulnerable secrets.

Let go of the old. Retain the new.

Let's relax and listen to the head. Listen to the face, the throat, the shoulders, the neck, the eyes, and the top of the head. Listen to the mind. Are your thoughts crowded or spacious? What is here in this moment? Relax resistances and stay attentive to whatever you feel.

Listen, receive.

Let go of the old. Retain the new.

Relax.

Let's relax and listen to everything all at once. Does anything in particular call your attention? What is here in this present moment? How do you feel in this present moment?

Relax and bring yourself to completion.

Did you learn anything about yourself in this practice?

Relax, Receive, Create

We have now established three very important practices: relax, receive, and create. Let's repeat them in order.

First, relax. Let it all go. Let go of your intentions and efforts. Allow yourself to drift without focus or restriction.

Second, receive. Listen to your sensations. Hear your emotions. Notice your thoughts. What messages are your gut, heart, and head sending you right now?

When you hear something new, take a moment to relax. Let go of the old. Ground yourself. Remember whatever might be new and important.

Third, create. Imagine yourself achieving an amazing goal. Feel what it would feel like to achieve this goal. Imagine how it would look and sound. Who are you in this imagination? What emotions accompany this imagination?

When you have imagined this goal with clarity, take a moment to listen. How do you feel? Then, take a moment to relax. Let go of the old. Ground yourself. Remember whatever might be new and important.

Relax. Feel your body as you breathe in. Let go as you breathe out.

Notice your body. Notice your environment. Come back to your baseline: refreshed, renewed, transformed.

Observational Practices

Observe Your Breathing

Let's think of breathing as a symbol. New air comes in. Old air goes out. Muscles exert effort to expand your lungs. Muscles relax as you exhale. Effort, relaxation. New, old.

Watch this phenomenon unfold. Notice how it feels. Anchor your attention to your breathing. Just watch your breathing and direct all your attention there. Become simple. Just watch. Nothing else. Just watch. Try this for a few minutes.

What does watching feel like?

What does the watcher feel like?

Observe Your Thinking

If you do not intend to think anything, do thoughts emerge unintentionally? Let's find out.

Watch your mind as a passive observer. Is your mind busy? Is it still? Does it feel excited? Anxious? Tired?

Are there any thoughts in your mind, or is there a stillness when you intend nothing but observation?

What does watching feel like?

What does the watcher feel like?

Witness in Freedom

First, observe an experience. Perhaps, observe an emotion, a thought, or a sensation. Then, take a step back and separate from the experience. Find freedom from it. Release the experience and watch it evolve. Let it evolve however it wants.

Feel and release.

Feel and release.

Find Stillness

Your environment may be noisy, or it may be quiet. Either way, you can focus on the sound, or you can focus on the silence. What happens when you focus on the silence? Is it calming? Clarifying? Deepening?

Your environment may be crowded or spacious. Either way, you can focus on the objects, or you can focus on the space. What happens when you focus on the space?

Your emotions may be tense or relaxed. What happens when you focus on relaxation?

A Sequence in Four Steps

Relax, Feel, Observe, Create

First, let's relax. Let go of what is unnecessary. Perhaps imagine all that is unnecessary flowing into the Earth.

Second, feel. Feel your body. Feel sensations, muscle tension or relaxation. Then, feel your emotions and your mind. How are you doing in this present moment?

Third, observe. Take a step back. Observe with freedom, non-attachment, and peacefulness. Simply notice your experience as it evolves and allow it to evolve.

Fourth, create. Imagine achieving a goal. Imagine a positive emotion that accompanies this goal. Imagine yourself achieving this goal and feeling this emotion.

Now, let's climb back down the ladder. Observe your emotions. Feel yourself as a witness. Feel your body. Free your emotions and allow yourself to feel them more deeply. Relax and release. Let go of what is unnecessary. Relax.

Now, notice your breathing. Notice your external environment. Relax lightly as you emerge into completion.

Release and Expression

People are often afraid to express their emotions. Crying is often seen as weak. Anger is often seen as dangerous. Unfortunately, these fears end up strengthening repressions and keeping emotions bottled up inside. Repressed emotions then become unconscious and problematic. Emotions are like messengers that persist in delivering their message until they are listened to. Repressed emotions will therefore cause you to suffer or act out in more and more extreme ways in the effort to be understood.

Sometimes, listening to our emotions internally is all that we need to do. However, other times, expression or release is also necessary.

As you gain experience with the practices in this book, you might have the opportunity to create bigger and more profound emotional shifts. As the intensity level rises, crying, laughing, or sighing are often needed forms of release.

Be respectful of others and how your expression might affect them. However, also know that sometimes your emotions need a way of being released into the external world. I encourage you to find healthy ways to cultivate emotional release: perhaps in structured, consensual containers with other people, perhaps through creating art, perhaps by letting it all out by yourself in a place where no one else will be offended, and so on.

Imaginative Practices

Simple Imagination

First, let's relax.

Now, imagine an empty space and place a simple shape in the center of it. You could imagine a black square, a green triangle, or perhaps a cube. Once you have selected your shape, commit to imagining it for the next couple of minutes. Attempt to imagine only this shape. Try not to allow your imagination to run away in unintentional directions.

If you experience difficulty with this, do not worry. This is, in fact, a very difficult task to master. If this exercise feels easy, see how much you can deepen the imagination, making it more clear, detailed, vibrant, and specific.

Notice your reactions as you imagine your simple shape. Feel your emotions and release what is no longer necessary. Breathe in and breathe out.

Relax.

Positive and Negative Imagination

First, let's relax.

Now, imagine an empty space. Fill the empty space with an imagination of achieving a goal and feeling a positive emotion. Add details to this imagination. Paint a picture, hear the sounds, or feel the sensations you desire. Clarify what you really want in this imagination and what it would feel like to get it.

Notice how this imagination makes you feel. Relax and release.

Clear your imagination. Now, create an imagination of failing to achieve the same goal you thought of earlier. Explore the negative emotions and details associated with this failure. What exactly has failed and why?

Observe how this imagination affects you. Relax and release.

Clear your imagination. Now, recreate the positive version of the imagination. Recreate the experience of achieving your goal and experiencing a positive emotion. Notice if there are any changes you want to make. Notice if your imagination can be deepened.

Can you answer the question, "What is important here?"

Feel your sensations, emotions, and thoughts. Relax and release.

Come back to the external world and bring your meditation to completion.

Imagine Something Unexpected

First, let's relax.

Now, imagine an empty space. Bring to mind an issue that concerns you. Imagine several outcomes regarding this issue that would be unexpected. Consider pathways into the future that you have never considered.

Let's end by creating a positive vision of the future unfolding. Feel a positive emotion and allow it to deepen into your soul.

If you want to, take a moment to describe your most important experiences with these imaginative practices in your journal.

Intention-Based Practices

An Emotion, Mindset, and Goal

This time, let's start by feeling our breath. Feel your body as you inhale. Relax all your effort and stress as you exhale.

Now bring to mind a positive emotion that you want to cultivate. It could be joy, love, peace, hope, excitement, inspiration, power, or any other pleasurable or useful emotion. Imagine feeling this emotion. Step into it. Intend to create and feel this emotion.

Notice your reaction. How does your body feel? Do any emotions arise as a response to your intention?

Relax and release.

Now, imagine living from a mindset that supports the emotion you chose to cultivate. It could be deep focus, empathetic communication, efficiency, forgiveness, creative intelligence or any other productive or useful state of mind. Imagine inhabiting this state of mind fully and deeply. Step into it. Intend to create and experience it.

Notice your reaction. How does your body feel? Do any emotions arise as a response to your intention?

Relax and release.

Lastly, imagine what kind of goals you could accomplish with the powerful emotion and mindset you have been developing. Create a scene in your mind or tap into other senses to deepen into your imagination. Imagine being who you need to be to accomplish these goals. Then, step into this identity. Create and feel it.

Notice your reaction. How does your body feel? Do any emotions arise as a response to your intention?

Relax and release.

Feel your emotions.

Relax and release.

Notice your breathing. Notice your external environment. Lightly relax as you bring yourself to completion.

Have you learned any lessons during this meditation? If you want to, write down any insights or ideas in your journal.

Overcome a Psychological Block

Let's begin by relaxing and releasing all that is old and unnecessary. Imagine any unnecessary tension flowing into the Earth. Perhaps imagine being in a beautiful, natural environment as you do this.

Now, imagine achieving a goal that you are having difficulty with. How will it feel to achieve this goal in your body? How will you feel emotionally? What state of mind will you be in? What kind of a person will you be?

As you go through these imaginations, notice any reactions that emerge. If a reaction does emerge, take a minute to explore what might be arising. Is this reaction a specific thought? Is it a certain flavor of emotion? What is the reaction trying to tell you?

Do any of these psychological blocks feel applicable to your situation?

I don't deserve this goal.

This goal is not possible for me.

This goal could cause harm to me or someone else.

This goal requires that I make a sacrifice that I'm not willing to commit to.

Question the thoughts behind any blocks that you discover and seek to uncover a deeper level of truth. Write down any important conclusions that you arrive at.

To find completion, spend another minute freely receiving your emotions and bodily sensations. Then, relax and release for another minute.

> *Using Imagination & Intention to Heal Blocks*
>
> Imagination and intention practices can be used to bring up and discover psychological blocks. By aiming your imagination at a specific goal, you can get in touch with all the blocks you have surrounding that goal. Once these blocks are in your awareness, relaxing, releasing, feeling, and observing practices can help you heal your relationship to these issues.
>
> This is one of the most important ways in which the practices we have covered so far are synergistic, becoming more powerful together than they are separately.

Bring Your Intention into Your Day-to-Day Life

Select an intention or goal that you have been working with in your meditations. Identify the core emotion associated with this intention or goal. Practice cultivating this emotion throughout your day and, especially, at times when you need this emotion as a resource or guide. At first, try bringing this emotion to mind as you perform simple activities like folding laundry or taking a walk. Then, bring this emotion into more and more of your life, forming a habit over time. Aim to eventually be able to call upon this emotion easily and powerfully whenever you need it.

In addition, spend some time reflecting on how this emotion can lead you into specific and useful action steps. Write your intentions in your journal and revisit them often if you find this to be a helpful supplement.

The Full Spectrum

Relax, Feel, Observe, Imagine, Intend

This practice progresses through five steps: relax, feel, observe, imagine, and finally intend. These five steps create a spectrum from more relaxing practices that cultivate greater awareness to more active and exciting practices that energize the spirit toward goals and important values. Taken together, these practices, in this order, paint a relatively complete picture of the inner processes of the psyche. Let's begin.

Relax – Exhale deeply and let go of any unnecessary tension. Let go of any unnecessary emotions. Let go of any unnecessary thoughts. Let go of any unnecessary intentions. Release your focus. Rest and drift.

Feel – Feel your body. Notice sensation, tension, and emotions. Relax as a way of feeling more deeply. Become vulnerable. Let your emotions in. Let go of anything that is unnecessary.

Observe – Take a step back. Watch your experience as it evolves. Release your experience and let it evolve as it wants to. Notice what you are watching and notice the watcher. Find freedom from all that you observe in the simple act of watching, feeling, and releasing whatever you find unnecessary.

Imagine – Imagine achieving a goal and the positive emotions that achievement will bring. Paint a scene, hear the sounds, and feel the sensations. Who are you in this imagination? What is important here? How can you align with the goal you want to achieve? Notice any reactions. Feel them and release them. Take note of any important information that they offer.

Intend – Intend to create the emotions and thoughts that support your goal. Commit to the action steps you need to take. Integrate them into yourself and resolve any conflicts. Notice any reactions. Feel them and release them. Take note of any important information that they offer.

To close your practice, bring attention back to your body. Relax and release. Notice your external environment and find completion. Write down any important insights you gained from your meditation.

Simple Alignment Method

We have now covered five primary practices: relax, feel, observe, imagine, and intend. Each of these practices has a unique function, and is best suited to address specific problems. If we can select the most beneficial practice for a given situation, we can customize and deepen our meditations in an important way.

In this section, we will learn a technique I call simple alignment method. As usual, let's begin with relaxation. Then, continually ask yourself if you are feeling stressed or ready to take on a new challenge. For our purposes, stress might include tiredness, negative emotions, overwhelm, confusion, or any number of other forms of "un-readiness."

If you are feeling ready, then move on to the next practice in the series – from relaxation to feeling to observation to imagination to intention. If you are feeling tired or stressed, then go to the previous practice in the series.

For example, if I start with relaxation and find that I'm feeling ready, I would then move to feeling. If I am still feeling ready, I would move on to observation. If I get a little tired, I would drop down to feeling. And if I continue to feel tired, I would drop down to relaxation. After a while, if I feel ready, I would begin to build back up again.

Try simple alignment method now, and, if you need to, refer to our five practices below:

1. Relax
2. Feel
3. Observe
4. Imagine
5. Intend

Meditate on the Four Elements

Earth

Relax. Imagine your bare feet on the natural ground. You and the Earth are connected.

Imagine everything you need to let go of flowing out of you into the Earth. Can you feel something like electricity or energetic potential in your body? If so, imagine releasing that energy and coming into balance with the Earth.

Imagine that all your stress and negativity are transferred into the vast, deep layers of ground beneath you. All that you release decomposes and breaks down into its fundamental components. Imagine all the resources of the Earth mixing together and new life springing from every corner of the world.

Imagine new energy and nourishment coming to you in the form of food, water, air, and everything else you need to thrive. The Earth supports you.

Now, imagine being the Earth. Imagine being solid, balanced, and without tension.

Water

Imagine being washed clean in cool, refreshing water. Imagine everything you need to let go of being washed away in the water.

Now, imagine yourself as water. Imagine how you would bend and morph into whatever shape comes most easily. Imagine all your rigidities being stretched and flexed like a session of emotional yoga.

Fire

Imagine all that you need to let go of being burned away. Imagine yourself as fire and feel the energy within. Cultivate your inner power.

Air

The fire fades away and spaciousness pervades everything in the aftermath. Imagine your being stretching across the vastness of the sky. In that spaciousness is potential and the beginnings of new creativity.

Where will you go from here?

Earth Transformed

Relax. Connect to the Earth. Flow into the ground and let the ground flow into you.

Relax and cultivate solidity.

Visioning Your Future
Part I

If your life progressed in an ideal manner, where would you want to be in ten years? Take a minute to write your answer in your journal.

To achieve these end goals, what milestones do you want to reach across these ten years?

What habits do you need to cultivate now and throughout these years on a daily basis in order to reach your end goals? List these habits in your journal.

If you are unsure about a goal or strategy, write it down anyway and make a note of your uncertainty. Consider this a brainstorming session, rather than a commitment.

You may want to consider categories like: career, finances, health and fitness, relationships, family, emotions, education and learning, adventure and fun, and so on.

Discovering Shadows

In this section, we will look at a few psychological systems. As we review the components of each system, we will search for your shadows – areas where you have repressions, unconsidered possibilities, and limitations.

The Integral Developmental Spectrum

Ken Wilber's Integral Theory provides a beautiful description of how we grow psychologically through childhood and into different stages of adult development.

I will briefly describe each stage in the Integral model. I will also add in some associations from Erik Erikson's developmental model and a bit of my own spin on things.

After reading each stage, write down any reactions you feel, including emotions, judgments, and physical responses.

Crimson – Survival, working to meet basic needs like the need for food, water, and shelter, life is physical and sensory here

Magenta – Tribe, family, bonding, our first impressions of trust and mistrust, the magical thinking of childhood

Red – The initial emergence of power and autonomy, learning to be your own person with your own desires and boundaries, ensuring your safety beyond the immediate, present moment

Amber – Tradition, mythical stories and moral parables, learning the value of cooperation, learning the value of structure, learning the wisdom of our ancestors

Orange – Reason and science, discovering your individual beliefs and uniqueness, learning to believe in yourself and your ability to understand the world, learning to work hard and intelligently

Green – Deeper love and connection, learning the value of free and diverse expression, learning to balance judgment with non-judgment or open-mindedness, learning to empathize with different perspectives

Teal and higher stages – The co-existence and integration of opposites, establishing big-picture hierarchies of value, cultivating a philosophical or spiritual sense of meaning, learning to live with integrity and working to contribute to the world

---

The Integral House Metaphor

It is overly simplistic to think of people as being "at" one stage of development. The reality is more like a house where each floor is a different developmental level. We are constantly working to build new rooms and floors in our house. However, we also have to maintain the parts of the house that have already been built. If something fails in the foundation, all the floors of the house might be affected.

Growth Steps

Take a look at each of the stages one more time and reflect on your personal history. Can you see yourself growing up through these stages? Do you have any interesting emotional reactions to any of these stages?

One excellent practice is to cultivate the virtues of every Integral level. If you find this exercise inspiring, try picking two or three virtues across the Integral spectrum that you want to develop. Then, imagine possessing these virtues more deeply and acting from these virtues more effectively. Notice any reactions. Relax, feel, and observe your way through any reactions as needed. Note any lessons learned in your journal.

Integral Resources

In this book, I have only included this brief introduction to Integral Theory. Integral Theory is elaborated upon not only in the thirty or so books published by Ken Wilber but also by numerous other authors and innovators.

You can check out the resources below for more in-depth explanations of Integral Theory.

integrallife.com/what-is-integral-approach

The Religion of Tomorrow, *A Brief History of Everything*, and other books by Ken Wilber

The Enneagram of Personality

The Enneagram is a deep system of personality and core motivations. The Enneagram consists of nine primary personality types. I will present short descriptions of these personality types below. As you read these descriptions, make note of any interesting reactions you have. Consider if any of these personality types sound like you or someone you know. Do any of these types of people create challenges for you?

Type One – The Reformer

Type ones believe in a set of values and will fight to uphold those values. Healthy ones are courageous, honorable, detail-oriented, and hardworking. On the other hand, ones can also run the risk of being perfectionistic, overly judgmental, critical, and rigid in situations that call for flexibility or adaptability.

Type Two – The Helper

Type twos focus on helping individual people and nurturing relationships. Healthy twos are caring, compassionate, and dedicated. Unhealthy twos can sacrifice their own health while trying to help others. They can also be manipulative or use "giving to get" style strategies. If their gifts are not appreciated or reciprocated, twos may become resentful.

Type Three – The Achiever or The Star

Type threes focus on achieving success in a way that others appreciate or admire. Healthy threes are inspiring, powerful, and incredibly hardworking. Unhealthy threes may lose their values and sense of identity in the pursuit of approval or shallow, surface-level images of success.

Type Four – The Romantic or The Individualist

Type fours focus on finding meaning and discovering their unique story. Fours may sometimes be withdrawn and have a tendency to look inward. However, they usually also have a desire to tell their story and be seen. Healthy fours are often amazing artists, storytellers, or soulful philosophers. Unhealthy fours may lose themselves in negative emotions, bringing other people down in the process. They might despair over the lack of ideal experiences in their life and become hopeless, overwhelmed, or envious.

Type Five – The Investigator

Type fives focus on intellectual pursuits, which may include projects of both a more practical or more philosophical nature. Type fives are the most introverted type and prefer to spend a lot of time studying and preparing before taking social or worldly action steps. Healthy fives can be incredibly innovative and might produce new academic advances or game-changing inventions. Unhealthy fives can become isolated, jaded, arrogant, and ungrounded as they disconnect from the social fabric of society.

Type Six – The Loyalist or the Guardian

Type sixes focus on developing security and preparedness for themselves and the groups they serve. Healthy sixes are great detail-oriented problem solvers. They are ready for any contingency, perceptive, funny, and committed to their tribe. Unhealthy sixes can be overly anxious and critical. They may limit themselves to black and white thinking when more greyscale approaches would be more effective.

Type Seven – The Enthusiast

Type sevens focus on living life to the fullest. They seek novel and superlative experiences like traveling all over the world or finding the best restaurant in town. Healthy sevens are fun to be around and excel at brainstorming or visioning ideas for the future. Unhealthy sevens may be scattered or uncommitted. Sevens might avoid or ignore the negative side of life while rigidly focusing on the positive.

Type Eight – The Challenger

Type eights focus on getting things done on a practical level. They focus on protecting and leading their tribe. Type eights have a powerful presence and don't mind conflict. Healthy eights offer strength, courage, and passion to their community. Unhealthy eights can be angry and may have trouble being vulnerable, even in situations where vulnerability is called for.

Type Nine – The Peacemaker

Type nines focus on creating harmony within their group or tribe. Healthy nines are empathetic, adaptable, wise, and often artistic. Nines are good communicators, meditators, and counselors. Unhealthy nines can lose their sense of identity while constantly accommodating others. Nines might repress their anger and may sink into depression or laziness.

Wings

Wings are a beautiful part of the Enneagram system. Wings teach us that adjacent types – for example type 2 and type 3 or type 9 and type 1 – are related. Your personality type may have a strong influence from one of your wings! My personality type is a 5 wing 4, meaning that I am primarily a 5 with some traits that resemble a 4.

Growth Steps

There are lots of growth steps you can take advantage of once you understand your Enneagram type and the system in general. For now, I invite you to focus on just three questions. In these three questions, let's think of each Enneagram type as a life strategy with potential advantages and disadvantages.

1. Can you empathize with the motivations behind all of the strategies across the Enneagram? Which types might you benefit from understanding better?

2. Which strategies would you benefit from using more?

3. Which strategies do you over-use or feel stuck with?

If you want to, write down your answers to these questions in your journal.

Enneagram Resources

There is a lot more to the Enneagram than the short introduction I've included here. If you are interested in going deeper into the Enneagram, my favorite book on the subject is *The Wisdom of the Enneagram* by Don Riso and Russ Hudson. There are also some great (and often very funny) YouTube creators dedicated to the Enneagram, such as Dr. Tom LaHue and Abbey Howe. If you are looking for funny videos, Top Knot Comedy with Leeann & Michelle is great!

Using the Enneagram for Relationships

The Enneagram is a wonderful tool for personal development, and it is perhaps an even better tool for *interpersonal* development. The Enneagram teaches us about perspectives other than our own, and this increases our empathy.

The practice on the next page is a method for two people to grow closer and see each other's worlds more deeply.

Using the Enneagram for Relationships

1. Identify the Enneagram type that fits your personality the best. Do the same with your partner. Note that people are easily mistyped, and you may need to do further research or consult with an expert to get to the bottom of the matter.

2. Discuss key ways in which your type and your partner's type differ. If it is difficult to understand why your partner would differ from you in a particular way, explore that topic with them and seek to uncover the core motivations at play. Can you guess at the motivations based on the Enneagram types that are involved?

3. Inquire about the broader implications of this conversation. Are there strategies that you have unnecessarily discarded? Are there judgments that you can now change or release?

Shadows in the Adoga Spectrum

Do you remember the progression of the five Adoga practices? Relax, feel, observe, imagine, and intend.

Each of these practices is associated with an aspect of life that you might have a shadow around.

Let's think about the mindset and potential shadows surrounding each practice. Notice your reactions as you read.

Relax

Does it feel unproductive to relax? How about lazy, gluttonous, shameful, or improper?

It may look like nothing productive is happening on the outside when we relax. However, relaxation is actually very important for growth. Through relaxation we become restored and empowered to embark on new adventures. A car with no fuel goes nowhere. Deep relaxation can offer gifts such as intuitive insights, emotional integration, and added potential energy which can then be directed to a chosen area of focus.

Feel

Experiencing and expressing emotions can be vulnerable and may expose painful subjects that are not pleasant to face. Nevertheless, feeling our emotions provides us with an important landscape of information. As I mentioned before, emotions are like messengers that persist in delivering their message until they are listened to. While these messages may not always be wise or correct, they do at times contain valuable information that you might not receive through any other pathway. When an emotion is not useful, it still needs to be listened to. Otherwise, the emotion will become a frustrated and repressed voice within you that will cause problems and deteriorate your inner harmony.

Observe

Observation involves stepping back and gaining a new perspective on your experience. If you can master the skill of noticing your experience while not attempting to control it, you can unlock a deep level of awareness and freedom. Giving up control in this way can be scary. Deep observation takes courage. It also takes patience. Observation is a confrontation with spaciousness, and this can seem boring and unpleasant. However, it is a useful confrontation. Spaciousness brings out the issues we need to focus on. We are all stuck in many habits and patterns that go unnoticed and unrecognized. Only through attentive observation can we become aware of these patterns and then become free of them.

Imagine

Imagination is the birthplace of our fears, but it is also the birthplace of our dreams. Imagination gives us hope. Daring to hope is scary, yet essential. Imagination offers a wonderous opportunity to explore and discover your purpose. Without the proper use of the imagination, we may end up depressed, lacking inspiring goals and strategies. Imagination is the key to moving forward into an exciting future worth sacrificing for.

Intend

Preparation is important, but ultimately we must take direct action steps to achieve our goals. If you want something, focusing on what you can do about it is the key to empowerment. Without a healthy relationship to intention, we may get stuck in endless planning, dreaming, wishing, or complaining. To become a master of intention is to become a master of your own destiny.

Growth Steps

Notice how the five practices in the Adoga spectrum form a process with a beginning, middle, and end. First, we gather resources and knowledge. Second, we free ourselves into new possibilities and discover a way forward. Finally, we work on our vision until it is a reality.

Do you get stuck at a particular point in this spectrum? Do you neglect the beginning steps and end up acting without enough resources or acting rashly without enough information? Do you neglect the later steps, constantly dreaming up plans but never taking direct action?

Make a note in your journal of any possible shadows you may have on the Adoga spectrum. Review the descriptions of the five mindsets above if necessary.

Visioning Your Future

Part II

Let's review your notes from each of the sections in the Discovering Shadows chapter. What are the most important insights you discovered? Are there any big-picture themes emerging? Can you briefly summarize two or three takeaways? Perhaps, you can even express one of these insights with a single word or phrase that you can easily remember. Are there any plans you want to make or action steps you want to take based on these insights?

Let's revisit your vision for the future. If you are inspired to do so, create a new vision that incorporates what you have learned recently.

The Emotions of the Adoga Spectrum

Alignment Method Based on Emotions

We previously discussed simple alignment method – the idea that we can select practices on the Adoga spectrum based on our inner sense of feeling stressed or ready to move forward.

We will now progress to a more detailed form of alignment method. In this version, we will select a practice based on a specific emotion we are struggling with or a specific emotion we are seeking to experience.

I will present emotions and emotional themes that are associated with each of the five practices – relax, feel, observe, imagine, and intend. Along the way, I'll also point out why each practice is best suited to address the emotions associated with that category.

With this framework, you will be able to customize your personal growth work based on the emotions that you need to work with. Once mastered, this is an incredibly powerful strategy.

Relax – Tiredness and Readiness

Relaxation is probably the simplest of these categories. Tiredness is the feeling that indicates you need to relax. Readiness is the feeling that indicates you should move on to more active endeavors. Simple as that!

Though, I should also mention that tiredness can take on many forms. Overwhelm and stress, for example, are more active types of emotions. However, they may still be good indicators that relaxation and recovery are called for.

Interestingly, boredom is a negative emotion that tells us we should move away from relaxation toward more active and exciting endeavors.

Feel – Hurt and Love

The feeling category is associated with fundamental and child-like emotions. On the negative side, these include hurt, hate, shame, guilt, and aloneness. On the positive side, these include love, joy, child-like enthusiasm, foundational energy, and connectedness.

In many developmental processes, we feel before we learn to observe, imagine, or intend. This category deals with the simple and intuitive understanding we develop from our earliest years. These emotions address basic questions like: Am I good or bad? Are you good or bad? Am I loved and cared for? And so on.

These emotions tend to go deep and be heart-centric.

I recommend you work with the feeling practice if you are struggling with hurt, hate, shame, guilt, or aloneness. This entails opening up to your negative feelings, allowing yourself to experience them fully, and then finally allowing yourself to release them. Through this process, listen to your emotions with genuine curiosity. Take note of any wisdom they offer and release any messages that are unhelpful.

I also recommend working with the feeling practice if you want to cultivate love, joy, or any of the other positive emotions associated with this category. Getting more in touch with your vulnerable, child-like, and heart-centric emotional space can open you up and allow light to shine through your soul.

Observe – Depression and Peace

Observation gives us the ability to focus. This is an amazing ability! We can channel our energy where we want it to go and concentrate our efforts in a specific and intentional way. However, focus also creates a potential for repression because we can focus away from something important.

Therefore, if you are struggling with repression, depression, or other forms of numbing, vibrance-destroying forms of sadness, observation may be a particularly helpful practice. By observing your breathing or another anchoring point of focus, we can learn to direct our attention in constructive and intentional ways. Simple objects of observation like breathing also put us in touch with spaciousness. Like a vacuum cleaner, spaciousness helps to pull away the old, the stale, and the unhelpful. Spaciousness has a way of bringing up whatever you need to hear and work on the most.

Master observers enjoy an immense peacefulness and appreciation for life. Master observers are comfortable with spaciousness and that creates peace. They also are present, focused, perceptive, and wise. These virtues arise from the awareness that one gains from careful and skillful observation. This kind of awareness also empowers them with the freedom to see and move beyond limiting habits and assumptions.

In summary, the practice of observation is best suited for alleviating depression and related forms of sadness while also cultivating peace and a clear, focused presence of mind.

Imagine – Fear and Inspiration

Fear, excitement, and inspiration all arise from our reactions to future possibilities. Our imagination is our tool for exploring future possibilities and is therefore the best suited practice for working through fears and cultivating excitement and inspiration.

In imaginative practices, we can explore fears, evaluate their validity, and formulate plans to defend against realistic dangers. We might discover that our fears are unfounded, which then frees us to let them go. We can also use the imagination to develop inspiring visions for the future. Through this process, we might gain insight into important values and strategies that may need to be included in our work.

Imagination is associated with excitement, inspiration, purpose, and moral integrity on the positive side as well as fear, obsession, unhealthy attachment, and greed on the negative side.

Intend – Anger and Power

When our intentions fail to achieve the results we desire, anger and frustration are the emotions that arise to inform us of the problems we are encountering. Anger and frustration may also want to communicate the importance of these problems and the correct way forward.

When our intentions succeed in realizing our goals, we feel power, confidence, satisfaction, and fulfillment. Such experiences serve as energizing proof of the effectiveness of our ideas and strategies. From this place, powerful emotions can serve as a resource as we extend our success to new heights.

Intention is the best suited practice to work through anger and cultivate a sense of empowerment because these emotions are direct responses to the intentions we are holding or the intentions we have set recently. When we are angry, we want to see a change in the world, but we feel powerless and perhaps trapped in our fixation on blaming others. The key to growth in this situation is to accept self-responsibility. You must either accept the situation as it is and release your negative emotions, or you must transform your negative emotions into empowering resources as you work to right the wrongs you perceive in the world. Intention-based practices help you to cultivate this kind of self-responsibility and self-empowerment.

Directions for Alignment Method

To practice alignment method based on emotions, follow these steps:

1. Relax.

2. Notice what emotions you are feeling.

3. Categorize your emotions based on the table on the next page.

4. Engage with the practice associated with the category that best describes your emotions.

5. Repeat.

If you feel inspired, try practicing alignment method for the next few minutes before moving on.

Practice	*Negative*	*Positive*
Relax	Tiredness Stress	Readiness
Feel	Hurt Hate Shame Guilt Aloneness Sadness	Love Joy Inner Child Enthusiasm Energy
Observe	Depression Hopeless Numbness Despair Grief Sadness	Peace Focus Appreciation Wisdom Freedom
Imagine	Fear Anxiety Obsession Paranoia	Inspiration Excitement Purpose
Intend	Anger Frustration Deprivation	Power Satisfaction Pleasure Fulfillment

Aligning with What You Want

One alternative method to the five steps outlined on page 72 is to focus on the practices that align with the positive emotions you most want to experience. In this approach, be sure to eventually include a mix of all the practices to experience the Adoga spectrum in full.

Relax, Feel, & Release More

In this section, we will return to some of the practices we began with and add additional layers of depth.

First, let's relax. Feel your body as you breathe in and relax as you breathe out.

To feel more, we must relax resistances that keep feelings away from our awareness. Do you feel any such resistances now? To release more, we must relax resistances that maintain attachments to old feelings and ideas. Do you feel any of these resistances now?

Feeling brings new things to us. Releasing lets old things move away from us.

In both, there must be movement. In both, there must be relaxation of all that prevents the movement.

I invite you to try deepening this movement. Allow yourself to flow. Letting the new arise. Letting the old fade.

Relax to feel. Relax to release.

As we feel and release, let us contemplate what might be ready to emerge and what might ready to be released. We will first consider each category of negative emotions in the Adoga spectrum.

Is there tiredness that wants to be felt? Is there tiredness that wants to be let go? Relax, feel, and release.

Is there hurt that wants to be felt? Is there hurt that wants to be let go? Relax, feel, and release.

Is there depression that wants to be felt? Is there depression that wants to be let go? Relax, feel, and release.

Is there fear that wants to be felt? Is there fear that wants to be let go? Relax, feel, and release.

Is there anger that wants to be felt? Is there anger that wants to be let go? Relax, feel, and release.

Let us now repeat this practice with positive emotions. It may seem strange to consider letting go of a positive emotion. However, remember that even positive emotions may distract us from important experiences that we need to feel and move on to.

To begin with, is there readiness that wants to be felt? Is there readiness that wants to be let go? Relax, feel, and release.

Is there love that wants to be felt? Is there love that wants to be let go? Relax, feel, and release.

Is there peace that wants to be felt? Is there peace that wants to be let go? Relax, feel, and release.

Is there inspiration that wants to be felt? Is there inspiration that wants to be let go? Relax, feel, and release.

Is there power that wants to be felt? Is there power that wants to be let go? Relax, feel, and release.

Notice how you feel now and what may have changed over the course of this practice. Notice your breathing. Notice your body.

Relax lightly as you emerge into completion.

The Psychology of the Adoga Spectrum

Alignment Method Based on Thoughts

Just as we can select practices based on the emotions we are struggling with or attempting to cultivate, we can also select practices based on thought patterns we are struggling with or attempting to cultivate. In this chapter, we will examine psychological problems and topics related to each category of practice – relax, feel, observe, imagine, and intend. I will present both positive and negative examples of thinking in each category.

This chapter and the next one will start to incorporate thinking tools into the emotional strategies that we have been building so far.

Using Relaxation as a Fun Foundation

How should we integrate work, fun, and rest? When it is possible, relaxation creates a foundation for a higher level of work. In this way, relaxation is like an investment in your own resources, and therefore is quite useful and productive in the long run!

This is a fun and enjoyable realization. It means that the joyful side of life can actually enhance the practical side of life. Too often we see the joyful and the practical as being in conflict, as if dedicating time to one takes away from the other. However, that mindset makes the mistake of ignoring the restorative and potentiating benefits of relaxation.

As you may have experienced throughout the practices in this book so far, relaxation is essential for releasing and integrating processes in personal growth. Relaxation also can deconstruct our repressions and put us in touch with valuable new intuitions and insights. Relaxation is therefore an integral part of our growth and progress.

Allow me to propose the following life philosophy surrounding relaxation: First, I do recommend taking care of your practical needs. If there is a fire, you are going to want to put it out before working on longer term strategies. But eventually, there will be opportunities to direct your attention beyond the most immediate of concerns. When those opportunities arise, create a fun foundation of relaxation. This means letting go of unnecessary stress and tension. When possible, build your potential energy through whatever you find fun, restful, and pleasurable! When it is time to work, don't succumb to overwhelm, needless anxiety, or despair. Simply, relax and then focus. Address your situation one step at time, with pleasant, peaceful, and attentive engagement.

By letting go of what is unnecessary through relaxation and energizing your priorities through focus, you can direct your attention efficiently and intentionally.

Just as we cycle through relaxing and creative practices in our meditations, you can cycle through mini-relaxations and productive strides forward in your communication, thinking, work, and various other endeavors.

You may find that phases of relaxation are useful for discovering new insights and ideas while phases of active engagement are useful for testing and implementation.

Feel Your Way to Forgiveness

Forgiveness is such an important topic, and yet immediately upon discussing it we run into the limitations of our current language and culture. Rules that hold people accountable are sometimes necessary. In this sense, forgiveness is not always the correct answer.

However, there is a type of emotional and inner forgiveness that is more or less always desirable. What I will call *emotional forgiveness* is the release of negative, hateful, or shaming emotions. Those negative emotions will cause you to suffer as long as you hold on to them. They are useful in one regard only: these negative emotions inform you about the nature and importance of a problem in your life. However, once you have listened to your emotions and understood their message, it is time to let them go. It is also important to acknowledge that an emotional message may be accurate or inaccurate, wise or unwise, rational or irrational. We want to listen to our emotions regardless so that we are aware of what's happening in our psyche. However, we must decide for ourselves if we believe the messages that our emotions deliver.

A simple practice for facilitating forgiveness is relaxing, deeply feeling your emotions, and releasing what is unnecessary. However, I also want to take this opportunity to present a more detailed and more intellectual forgiveness practice, which I call Five Step Forgiveness. This is a process for understanding and growing from mistakes. You can use this process to address feelings of shame and guilt directed toward yourself or feelings of blame and anger directed toward others. You may also use this process for situations that involve a combination of shame and blame. As you go through the steps below, you may want to consider how both emotions could be involved.

Five Step Forgiveness

Step One – Notice the Shame or Blame & Feel It

The first step is to recognize that you feel shame or blame and to gain an initial level of clarity around why. Perhaps you aren't sure, and that's okay. Simply describe to yourself what you are feeling and what you know about the origin of that feeling. See if you can identify one core mistake that your emotions are responding to.

As you describe your feelings and your situation, see if you can open up to your emotions. Notice how your body feels. Invite your emotions to reveal themselves in their fullest form. Feel as much as you can handle. Release what you feel comfortable releasing.

Step Two – How could you be better?

If you are experiencing shame, is there an actionable change that would improve this situation? If not, what's the use in holding on to this emotion? Perhaps, it is time to let it go. If there is a change you want to make, let's start making concrete plans and brainstorming some action steps.

If you are experiencing blame, what is your own role in the situation? What can you take responsibility for? Is there anything that you can do to make the situation better? If not, what's the use in holding on to this emotion? Perhaps, it is time to let it go. If there is a change you want to make, let's start making some concrete plans and brainstorming some action steps.

Step Three – How could the world be better?

If you are experiencing shame, did other people or the world at large also play a role in this mistake? What do you blame others for? Is there anything you can do to improve this situation? If not, maybe it is time to let go of your emotions.

If you are experiencing blame, can you specifically identify the mistake that you are seeing and what the solution is? If so, can you turn this problem into a project? Can you contribute to the world by fixing this problem? Do you want to work on fixing this problem? If not, maybe it is time to let go of your anger and frustration surrounding this situation.

Step Four – An Emotional Path Forward

If you have decided on some action steps, can you create positive and supportive emotions to help you in this process? What is the ideal emotional state to be in while taking these steps? Perhaps, consider transforming anger and blame into peace and power. Let's imagine successfully taking the steps you have decided on while feeling supportive and positive emotions.

Regardless of your decision to make changes or not, let's now release any unnecessary or harmful emotions. Practice feeling, grounding, relaxing, and releasing. Let go of what no longer serves you. Let breathing help you release.

Step Five – A Practical Path Forward

With a good emotional state to support you, revisit your action plan, if needed. Specify any helpful details and, when you are ready, commit to your plan.

If you did not decide to take on any action steps so far, consider if you might want to make some commitments around your own emotional self-care. Perhaps you want to repeat some kind of releasing practice to help you move on from this issue.

Observe Your Way to Hope and Vast Possibility

Let's introduce this section with a practice:

Relax. Release what is unnecessary. Ground yourself.

Now, observe your breathing for a few minutes. Notice the spaciousness. Notice what comes up. Notice what you are watching and notice the watcher.

Now, I invite you to join me in meditating upon the vastness of the universe. Consider the billions of years in our past that scientists can see back into. Did you know that scientists estimate that there are at least one hundred billion stars in our galaxy? We orbit around only one of those hundred billion stars. Did you know scientists have evidence of two trillion galaxies in the universe? And that's just what we can see right now. As large as our planet is, it is but a tiny speck in the vastness of what we can see.

Consider how many types of life there are on this planet alone. Consider how many human lives have been lived here on Earth. Consider how many subjects have been studied in great detail. Consider how many civilizations have risen from nothing and fallen away. How many have experienced joy, sorrow, and the birth of new life? How many have passed away?

What a grand stage we inhabit! How much there is to explore! The possibilities are endless if we allow them to be.

When we are ashamed and our emotions are limiting and negative, we reduce our connection to the beautiful and wonderous possibilities of life. When we believe in our own potential, life is revealed before us in all its dazzling complexity, and it invites us to come play.

Play can become passionate work. And passionate works can become important forms of progress as well as important contributions to other people's lives.

Where have you been limiting yourself? Gaze upon the infinite possibilities and imagine what could be out there waiting to be explored, who you could be, what gifts you could give and receive.

This is the meaning of life, or rather the incredible web of many forms of meaning – exciting, beautiful, and diverse! This is why we live and why gratitude is the only appropriate response to the deeply aware view of the world.

Let us watch our breathing once again. Now, notice the potential for all that in the observer and the observed.

Imagine and Intend Your Way to the Future

The vastness of the universe is beautiful and majestic, but, on its own, it can be paralyzing. Where do we go in this vast territory? What should we prioritize? What is our purpose? How should we focus our energy?

These questions are best answered through the creative imagination supported by the awareness of relaxing, feeling, and observing.

Spend a minute journaling about what makes you feel the most excited and inspired. Notice your emotional and physical reactions as you investigate this question. What have you encountered that feels the most important? Then, take a minute to consider how you can work on these important and exciting topics more. What goals do you want to set in these areas? What goals would you set if you really let yourself dream big?

If those goals feel overwhelming or scary right now, that's okay. For now, just focus on identifying the most important end points. Over the course of the rest of the book, we will be introducing strategies to break your goals down into manageable parts and proceed forward with an exciting form of confidence. Before we chart a specific path forward though, we need to know where we are going. If you are not sure where you want to go at this point, that's okay. Just choose a short-term experiment. Picking a direction forward is usually better than doing nothing, even if you have to adjust your direction down the road.

Once you have selected a set of goals, focus on both emotional and practical intentions. Identify key emotions that support your goals. Make a habit of imagining and intending these emotions in dedicated meditations as well as throughout your daily activities when that's feasible.

A Summary for Alignment Method

If you are working with themes of forgiveness, blame, and shame, consider spending some extra time with the feeling practice. If you are working with themes of hope, possibility, and freedom, consider using both observational and imaginative practices. Go to imaginative practices particularly when dealing with specific fears and goals. If you are working with themes of positive focus and empowerment, consider using intention-based practices.

Intellectual Practices and Techniques

Chunking Big and Small

Many people could achieve much bigger goals if they mastered the skill of chunking.

Chunking is an idea I first heard about from Tony Robbins. I've thought about it on my own since then and may have added a piece of originality here or there. The idea goes something like this:

When you create a plan to achieve a goal, you can create that plan with any number of steps. For example, let's say you want to write a book. You could create a plan with many steps:

1. Research book writing computer programs.

2. Choose a program.

3. Install the program or programs on your computer.

4. Evaluate if you have chosen the best program.

5. Begin researching the given topic.

6. Take notes on the research.

7. Evaluate what especially important subtopics need to be researched.

8. Create a summary of the notes.

9. Start to contemplate a focus.

10. Test different expressions of the focus.

With ten steps, we haven't even written a single word of the book. We were just barely starting to get a sense of what the project might be about. This kind of planning is too detailed. It feels discouraging because of the number of steps involved. With so many steps to mentally process, it seems like the endeavor is very long and difficult.

Let's compare this to the other extreme. We could also plan our writing process like this:

1. Brainstorm.

2. Write a draft.

3. Edit.

At first, this version might feel like a relief compared with the previous version, but it brings in a new kind of stress. With so little detail, each step can seem too big to accomplish. It leads us to give up, saying "How am I supposed to do this?" The first version was stressful because there were too many steps. This version is stressful because the steps are too big.

The balance point between these two extremes might look something like this:

1. Get broad exposure to the topic of interest.

2. Find a specific inspiration.

3. Research any missing relevant information.

4. Outline a version of the book.

5. Write a rough draft.

6. Edit for ideas.

7. Get feedback from others about the ideas.

8. Incorporate new thoughts from yourself and others into a revised draft.

9. Edit the revised draft for language.

10. Go through the final refining and publishing process.

This version is long enough to provide some ideas about how to accomplish the goal, but short enough not to be overwhelming.

The lesson here is to consider the number of steps you have "chunked" a project into. While all the above plans for writing a book might be technically accurate, the third one has a psychological advantage over the previous two. So, ask yourself, "Am I dealing with the right number of chunks for this problem?" And, if needed, try rechunking to produce a more helpful conceptual map or plan. The ideal is for a single step to feel challenging but doable. We also want the total number of steps to feel doable.

This simple tool can help you set bigger and better goals, while staying committed to your path of purpose and passion.

Probability and Logical Fallacies

I'll always remember this video where an audience member asked Elon Musk what he thought about the idea that we are living in a simulated universe constructed by someone or something else. This is similar to saying that we are living inside a virtual reality or videogame that is advanced enough to appear like the complex world we see around us. After laying out his argument, Elon responded by saying that he thought the odds were one in billions that we are living in "base" or original reality.

The audience member then says, "So, the assumption then is that somebody beat us to it, and this is a game."

Elon proceeds to double down on his idea, saying, "No, no, there's a one in billions chance that this is base reality."

The audience member says, "Oh, okay. What do you think?"

Elon doubles down again saying, "Well, I think it's one in billions."

When I first saw that clip, I learned an important lesson. The audience member was essentially asking Elon to round his answer into one of two simple categories: either we live in a simulated reality, or we don't. However, Elon refused to round off even the probability of one in billions into a certain answer. Doing this maintains the true complexity of the problem. However, many would be tempted to simplify their perspective so that it feels easier to deal with.

This is the philosophy I've developed since watching this video:

If you want to think at the highest level, think in terms of a spectrum of probability rather than in terms of black and white answers about how the world works. Consider what makes a weak argument and what makes a strong argument. Allow strong arguments to influence your probabilities a lot and allow weak arguments to influence your probabilities a little. This way of approaching the world can feel unsettling because it requires continuously facing uncertainties. However, this is the most honest and accurate approach.

Based on your map of probabilities, you of course have to make concrete choices. You will have to spend time with certain friends and not others. You will have to invest in certain career paths or projects and not others. These choices may require betting all your resources on a particular path. However, in the process of coming to a decision, it is best to build the most accurate map of probabilities that time allows.

In addition, studying logical fallacies can help you to understand what things should not be influencing your probability map very much or at all. Interestingly, many logical fallacies contain a little bit of truth, just not very much of it. For example, appeal to authority is a common logical fallacy in which someone argues that because an authority figure says something it must be true. This is a fallacy because, in fact, authority figures often make mistakes or might be lying. However, there may be a kernel of truth in the idea that someone with authority is likely to be in that position because of skills or expertise that make them more likely to arrive at the right answer. This is an example of a weak argument or a line of reasoning that might influence your probability map a little but should not be relied upon.

In contrast, some arguments should not change your probability map at all. For example, consider this logical fallacy, referred to as begging the question or circular reasoning.

The word of Zorbo the Great is flawless and perfect. We know this because it says so in The Great and Infallible Book of Zorbo's Best and Most Truest Things that are Definitely True and Should Not Ever Be Questioned.

-Example taken from yourlogicalfallacyis.com

In this example, a claim is made, but no valid support is offered. Therefore, the claim should not have any effect on our probability map.

Understanding these kinds of logical fallacies are a great way to improve your thinking skills! If you are inspired, I encourage you to learn more at websites like: yourlogicalfallacyis.com

Don't Throw the Baby Out with the Bathwater

I often learn from people that I largely disagree with. If I disagree with two-thirds of a book but the remaining third is something useful that I hadn't thought of, I would say that is a really good book.

People often reject an entire author, book, perspective, community, or style because of specific problems or negative experiences that in fact only characterize a small percentage of what they end up rejecting. Just because you had a bad Thai dish one time, do not reject all Thai food. Just because you don't enjoy the first chapter of a book, don't immediately disregard the whole book.

Similar to Elon's probabilities, this approach maintains more complexity at the cost of more time and effort. You do have to pick your battles. However, it is also important to be conscious about how you are simplifying the full picture for the sake of time.

By embracing many sources of information and sorting out the strengths and weaknesses of each source, you will end up with a richer understanding. If you reject things based on limited experience, your world will become small.

Thinking For Yourself

We necessarily outsource much of our thinking. It is not possible to be an expert in everything. So, we all specialize in different areas and collaborate. In this way, society becomes more than the sum of its parts. However, the problem is figuring out who to trust and when. Experts can be wrong or immoral. They can lie about being experts to begin with. So how do we proceed? We will have to research the experts enough to know if we can trust them, and we will have to research their field of study enough to understand the situation to some degree. But now, will we end up back where we started, needing to research everything on our own?

The answer I believe is to choose priorities to investigate, and not just one or two specialties. If something is very important, I recommend doing the work it takes to be able to think for yourself. That process will, of course, involve listening to experts. However, it will also involve mustering up the discipline and courage to do some intellectual work yourself. Because this is certainly labor-intensive, you will have to allow non-priority subjects to go relatively unstudied. In these areas, you may have to rely more on the judgment of others. However, always remember to hold a greater degree of uncertainty around these shadowy, unexplored topics. Do not presume to have answers to questions that you have not put effort into understanding. Despite the inevitable fear of the unknown, admit what it is that you do not understand.

Search for the Opposite

If you arrive at an answer to a question, look for opposing answers that may also be beneficial. This strategy will help you to eliminate blind spots and increase the breadth of your understanding.

For example, if you arrive at the conclusion that love is the most important of all virtues, consider what opposing viewpoints may also have some truth that you want to integrate. Look for valuable and reasonable opposites here. Proposing hate or ambivalence as important virtues does not make any sense. However, what about virtues like passion, discernment, or creativity? These virtues seem to offer a different perspective and could also be valuable contributions. By creating an integration of these types of diverse and important ideas, we can arrive at a place of greater wholeness and empowerment.

After identifying a set of answers to a question, you can then work on combining these answers together. You may find that the answers conflict with each other. Is one answer relevant only in certain situations? Is there an ideal balance point between two answers? Does the balance point change depending on circumstances?

Discovery Journaling

The discovery process generally begins with lots of little experiences and experiments. It generally ends with a small set of important conclusions. Interestingly, the best way to explain something is usually the reverse: start with your most important conclusions and then delve into the details.

I use my journal to discover things about myself and to do that I use a specific practice that I want to share with you.

1. Write down anything that seems (even mildly) important or interesting. Allow this step to be messy and disorganized. Flow with your stream of consciousness and don't enforce any kind of high standards at this point. You don't even have to fully understand what you are writing at this stage.

2. Review what you wrote in step one, along with any other old journal entries you care to revisit. Write a summary of the important parts of everything you are reviewing. Work on making this version a little more organized. Focus on the important priorities and leave out the less important or less accurate parts of previous entries.

3. Repeat the second step until you have a concise and clear expression of your insights.

These steps can be completed in one sitting or over the span of months and years. Although it may seem simple, this is a powerful, creative process.

I invite you to use this discovery process on the journal entries you have accumulated so far while working your way through this book. Review your thoughts and iteratively organize them into more and more succinct and valuable insights.

Integration

Formulating Your Constitution

Defining your values is an important milestone in one's development. And it's a milestone that needs to be repeated and updated as we grow. What is important in life? What do you aspire to? What principles do you want to make sure that you enact in your life? What principles are the most important? Is it love? Or passion? Or contribution or creativity or understanding or growth?

Write a short summary of your values in your journal if this activity appeals to you. Consider this your constitution and aim to live up to these values to the best of your ability.

You might also want to add some rules and guidelines for your life. For example, one of my rules is that I do not allow myself to make important decisions when I'm tired or in a negative emotional state (unless it truly is an emergency, and a decision must be made now). That's a pretty simple rule, but it has an important guiding influence on my life. Try to keep your constitution simple and succinct so that it is easy to remember and enact.

Relax and Create

Our journey is coming to a close now. We explored practices, insights, and plans for an inspiring future. There is a lot to integrate here. So, let's take a moment to come back to the simple practices that we started with.

Relax. Imagine anything old, stale, or unnecessary flowing out of you and into the Earth. Imagine the Earth supporting and nourishing you.

Breathe. Feel your body as you breathe in and relax as you breathe out.

Invite your emotions in. Relax and release the emotions that are ready to go.

Observe your breathing as it flows in and out. Notice what you are watching and who is watching. Notice the spaciousness.

Now, imagine a vast empty space. Clear your imagination. Then, bring to mind the new and exciting goals that you have been developing. See yourself achieving these goals and feeling the positive emotions that would accompany those accomplishments.

Notice your reaction to these imaginations. Observe your feelings and thoughts. Notice the observer. Feel your emotions and sensations. Relax. Release. Ground.

Come back to your imagination once again. Focus on the most important positive emotion that you want to carry with you.

Intend to create this emotion now and bring it with you into all your endeavors.

Relax.

Making It Physical

To solidify and deepen your growth, try out these strategies.

Body Posture – Imagine what kind of body posture and body language align with your goals. Try putting your body in that posture and see how it feels. If you like it, make it a habit!

Create a Beautiful Environment – Imagine what kind of environment would support and inspire your visions. How do you want your house, office, and various living spaces to look and be organized? Consider how you can imbue your environment with reminders of your goals and values.

Make It a Social Habit – If you are starting a new habit, social groups and recurring events can help!

Make Art – Can you capture your values or goals in art, story, or music?

Make It Happen – And, of course, the only mandatory strategy is:

Work on your goals and make it happen.

Visioning Your Future
Part III

We have already spent a lot of time contemplating, thinking through, and feeling into your future in this book. However, before we close, I want to offer one more opportunity to write a final vision in your journal.

Consider the entry you wrote in Visioning Your Future Part I. See how things have changed through the process of reading this book. Check over the key insights that you've written down. Are all of the important, new ideas you've learned about included in this vision? Do you want to expand upon your plans and action steps? Are there some new details to fill in?

I encourage you to write a more polished and organized version of your vision. Make this the official version. If you so choose, years from now, you'll be able to revisit this vision and ponder the effect that it has created in your life.

Good luck with your adventures.

Conclusion

The Resilient Mantra

My growth journey has been difficult and painful at times. All people have their struggles, even when they seem perfect and put-together on the outside. However, these challenges are no reason to give up on life. As Henry Ford told us at the beginning of this book, "Failure is only the opportunity more intelligently to begin again." Life becomes meaningful through the effort and journey of pursuing our goals and learning along the way.

Emotional practices like the ones I've shared in this book can make us feel really good, and it's important to feel good. However, when we strive to achieve goals in the real world, it takes more than happy feelings to produce success. It takes hard work, resilience, and the ability to gracefully contend with and learn from failure.

If we can combine hard work, emotional intelligence, and thinking skills, we can become both powerful and wise. If we can grow both on the inside and the outside, we can achieve extraordinary things of unknown limits. The vast world awaits your creativity.

Thank you for reading.

The Inspirations of Adoga

There is a deep thought process and philosophy behind Adoga. If you're interested in more details, I invite you to check out my book *Adoga: A Science and Spirituality of Profound Patterns* as well as my website projectado.com where I publish information about all my various projects.

In case you are curious how I arrived at the word "Adoga," I will share a brief summary of the term's origin.

During 2015 and 2016, I went on an inner journey and discovered the value of many personal growth practices. During that time, I transformed my relationship to my emotions. My struggle with depression dissolved. My creativity surged. My inner sense of peace deepened, and my joy exploded. Inspired by many spiritual and psychological teachers, I began to create my own method of personal growth which I named Adoga.

Adoga is an acronym that stands for Archetypal Divisions of Oneness Growth Activity. That's quite a complicated mouthful, I know. However, we can break down its meaning into a few key ideas. First, Adoga works with archetypes, which are simply big-picture patterns. Second, we can view these archetypes or big-picture patterns as the most foundational divisions or categories. Third, we can view these foundational divisions as creating initial separations in *oneness* – which is a conception of the universe as one, interconnected thing. Fourth, we can use these archetypes for our personal growth. Fifth, growth requires us to participate in activities or personal growth practices.

You can see the use of archetypes throughout this book in structures like the five primary Adoga practices: relax, feel, observe, imagine, and intend. I also consider the big-picture patterns of the Enneagram types or the Integral developmental levels to be archetypes. Models or frameworks like these can be incredibly valuable because they give you big-picture maps. They show you where problems and solutions may exist in the vast expanse of life's possibilities. The integration of the many perspectives offered by these archetypal systems can produce profound balance, harmony, wholeness, and empowerment.

Acknowledgments, Sources, and Gratitude

Derek Meyer served as the copyeditor for this book. Thank you so much, Derek! You offered many helpful suggestions that improved this book.

Danny Phelps gave me feedback on my content and ideas. I really appreciate the enthusiasm that you shared with me and the confidence that enthusiasm sparked within me. Thank you, Danny!

My mom, Lynn Haas, also gave me important feedback on my writing. Thank you for your clarity and discerning perspective.

My partner, Jaime Zoltick, has been helping me to develop and refine the Adoga practice. She also gave me useful insights into the simplification process. Thank you for your love and inspiring sense of vision!

The cover art was inspired by artwork created by Kesenia Ashland. The symbol you created has become very meaningful to me. Thank you!

The following works helped to inspire this book, and I have quoted directly from a few of them. Much gratitude to the creators of these books, videos, and webpages.

My Life and Work

by Henry Ford

Avatar: The Last Airbender

Book 2, Episode 9: "Bitter Work"

The Wisdom of the Enneagram

by Don Riso and Russ Hudson

The Complete Enneagram

by Beatrice Chestnut

Enneagram Basics

by Herb Pearce

Enneagram Beyond the Basics

by Herb Pearce

Enneagram YouTube Channels including Dr. Tom LaHue, Abbey Howe, and Top Knot Comedy with Leeann & Michelle

Many resources about Integral Theory including *The Religion of Tomorrow* by Ken Wilber and *A Brief History of Everything* by Ken Wilber.

Reinventing Organizations

by Frederic Laloux

Erik Erikson's Stages of Development

Erikson's stages are discussed in books such as *The Life Cycle Completed*. This article from verywellmind.com is also a good summary of the concept:

https://www.verywellmind.com/erik-eriksons-stages-of-psychosocial-development-2795740

Tony Robbins' perspective on chunking:

https://www.tonyrobbins.com/productivity-performance/power-of-chunking/

Is life a video game? | Elon Musk | Code Conference 2016

https://www.youtube.com/watch?v=2KK_kzrJPS8

yourlogicalfallacyis.com

The works of Carl Jung such as *Archetypes and the Collective Unconscious*

Check out Ryan's other books and projects at:

projectado.com

Join our community at:

depthandconversation.com

www.ingramcontent.com/pod-product-compliance
Lightning Source LLC
Chambersburg PA
CBHW020541080526
44583CB00013B/938